THE LITTLE
SPACECRAFT
THAT COULD

New Horizons' amazing journey
to Pluto and Arrokoth

Joyce Lapin

Illustrated by
Simona Ceccarelli

STERLING CHILDREN'S BOOKS
New York

"Five . . . four . . . three . . . two . . . one . . ."

At *"Liftoff!"* the spacecraft let her launch
system carry her skyward. She was gunning to
be the first spacecraft ever to fly to Pluto!

Pluto was so far from Earth that scientists knew hardly anything about it. Even the strongest telescopes could only see a fuzzy dot.

Still, people loved this little planet! Maybe because it was so distant and mysterious. Or maybe because it had the same name as a famous dog who hung out with a mouse.

Pluto's average distance from Earth is 3.7 billion miles. If you could fly there in a jet, it would take you 700 years. If you could *bike* there, it would take *47,000* years!

Pluto is in a part of the solar system called the *Kuiper Belt*. (*Kuiper* rhymes with *piper.*) This is a "ring" of millions of small objects that orbits the Sun even farther out than Neptune.

The little spacecraft had a name, too: *New Horizons*. This was a brave-sounding name, the spacecraft thought. And you *had* to be brave to fly to the edge of the solar system!

Just minutes after takeoff, *New Horizons* reached outer space. Her first-stage engine finished its fuel and she let it fall away. It was as natural as slipping off an empty backpack.

Her second- and third-stage engines kicked in, and then they too dropped away, leaving the spacecraft no bigger than a small piano. Light and free, she streaked through space at more than 10 miles per second.

EARTH   MOON   PLUTO

Pluto is 1,485 miles wide, making it smaller than the Moon. But a moon isn't a moon because of its size; it's a moon because it orbits a planet instead of the Sun.

Solid rocket boosters

First-stage booster

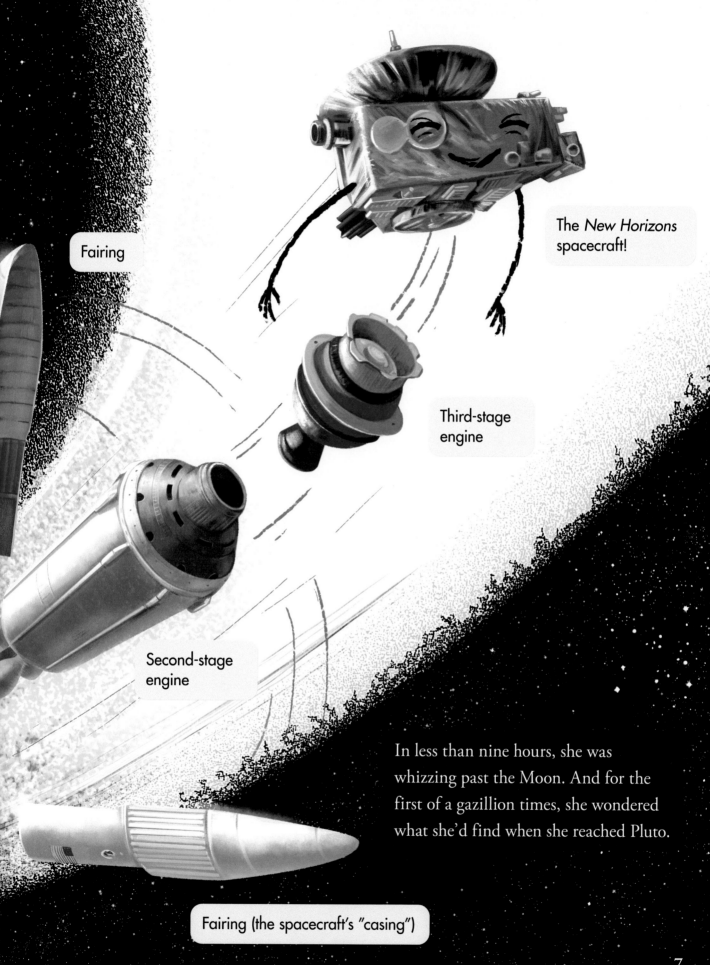

Fairing

The *New Horizons* spacecraft!

Third-stage engine

Second-stage engine

In less than nine hours, she was whizzing past the Moon. And for the first of a gazillion times, she wondered what she'd find when she reached Pluto.

Fairing (the spacecraft's "casing")

7

What was distant Pluto made of? What color was its sky? Were there lava-spewing volcanoes? Were there gross creepy-crawly things?

No one knew the answers, but everyone wanted to! So *New Horizons* was going to fly three billion miles to Pluto, collect close-up pictures and other kinds of data, and send everything back to Earth.

New Horizons was "robotic," which meant she carried no astronauts—and this was quite sensible, since she wouldn't be returning home. Once her mission was completed, she'd continue traveling outward and eventually leave the solar system.

And the little spacecraft was off to an awesome start! She'd blasted off on January 19, 2006—leaving Earth faster than any spacecraft ever built—and was zooming through the solar system at 36,000 miles an hour. Even at speeds like this, it would take nearly 10 years to reach Pluto. But the 2,500 men and women who designed, built, and launched her had prepared her for almost anything.

Except for what happened on August 24, 2006 . . .

Back on Earth, astronomers had been quibbling about Pluto. Some of them felt Pluto wasn't big enough to be called a planet. Now, seven months after *New Horizons* left her launchpad, astronomers suggested Pluto should be called a *dwarf planet*.

There used to be no real definition of *planet*—it was simply a "You'll know it when you see it" kind of thing.

But in 2006, astronomers changed this without consulting planetary scientists—scientists who actually *specialize* in planets. These experts (*and the Pluto-loving public!*) strongly disagreed with the astronomers' definition.

For planetary scientists, it was and remains clear: *If it's round, massive enough, and orbits a star, it's a planet.*

Well, this stung a bit. Pluto was *New Horizons'* reason for being! The spacecraft felt more determined than ever to complete her mission. And she was about to get help from the largest planet in the solar system.

The solar system's most well-known dwarf planets:

PLUTO   ERIS   CERES   HAUMEA   MAKEMAKE

There are more than 100 dwarf planets in the solar system. Most of them are in the Kuiper Belt with Pluto—but one of them, *Ceres*, is in the *asteroid belt*, a ring of rocky objects that orbits the Sun between Mars and Jupiter.

Gravity causes objects to "pull" on each other—and an enormous object like Jupiter has a very powerful pull. Like all planets, Jupiter is always racing around the Sun. *New Horizons'* team wanted her to be *pulled along with Jupiter*, to add some of its speed to her own. Astronomers call this a "gravity assist."

The planet Jupiter is so ginormous that 1,300 Earths could fit inside it!

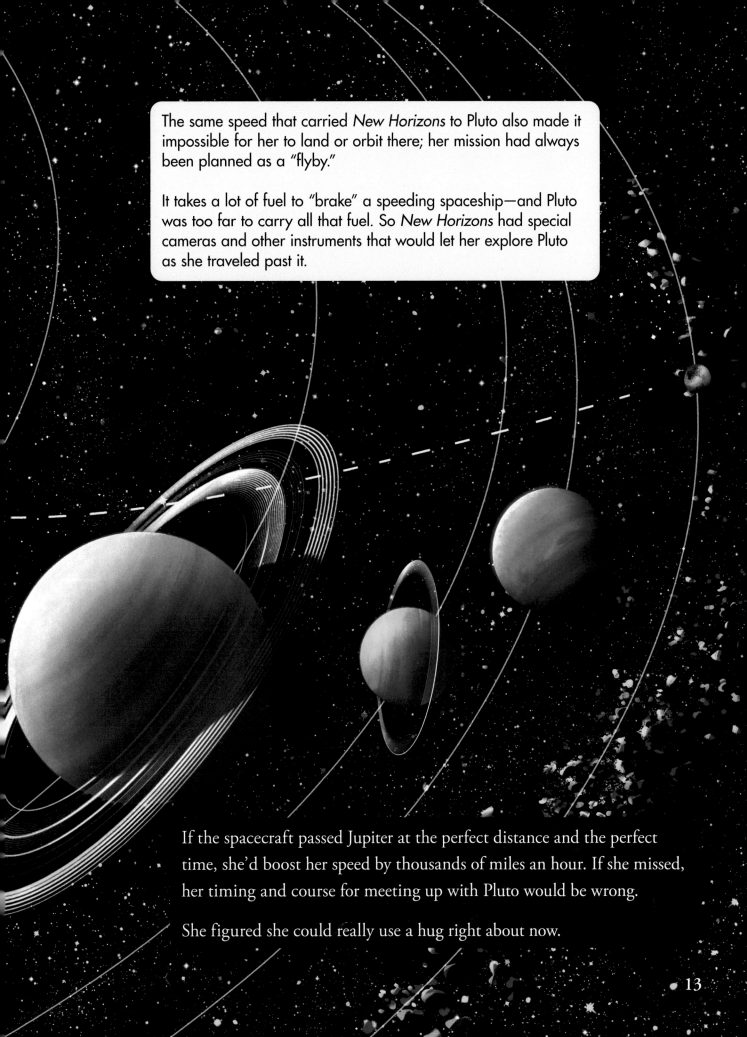

The same speed that carried *New Horizons* to Pluto also made it impossible for her to land or orbit there; her mission had always been planned as a "flyby."

It takes a lot of fuel to "brake" a speeding spaceship—and Pluto was too far to carry all that fuel. So *New Horizons* had special cameras and other instruments that would let her explore Pluto as she traveled past it.

If the spacecraft passed Jupiter at the perfect distance and the perfect time, she'd boost her speed by thousands of miles an hour. If she missed, her timing and course for meeting up with Pluto would be wrong.

She figured she could really use a hug right about now.

Carefully, she maneuvered to within 1.4 million miles of Jupiter. That may not *seem* very close—but you don't mess with a planet whose name means "King of the Gods."*

*Asteroids and comets often crash spectacularly into Jupiter, because of the planet's tremendous size and gravity.

Before the little craft knew it, she was being pulled along faster and faster by Jupiter. She wondered if it was proper for a $700 million spacecraft to think . . . WHEEEEEE!

Then at just the right time, she broke away from Jupiter and barreled out toward Pluto at nearly *a million miles per day*.

All the planets except Earth are named after mythical gods and goddesses. Because Pluto is so far from the Sun, it was named for a god who lived in a very cold, dark place. The name was suggested by an 11-year-old girl from England who knew a lot about mythology.

The little spacecraft was ecstatic; she'd rocked the trickiest part of her voyage! It was still another 2.5 billion miles to Pluto, but she'd do what everyone does on a long trip: she'd nap.

Technically, *New Horizons* would *hibernate*. This meant she'd shut down most of her systems and travel on "autopilot" for most of the next eight years. Doing this would help keep her computers and instruments like new.

For most of the spacecraft's trip, she used no fuel! The speed from her *launch* was a gift that kept on giving.

On Earth, flying objects rub against air, and this "air resistance" makes the objects slow down. But outer space has no air, so there's no air resistance—and once an object's moving, it simply *keeps* moving.

Once a week (in her sleep!) she'd send a signal to Earth, just to let her team know that she was okay. And every few months, the scientists would "wake her," to give her new instructions and check her systems.

All told, *New Horizons* hibernated for two-thirds of her journey. In 2008, she glided peacefully past the orbit of Saturn—though the ringed planet was elsewhere in its orbit at the time—and in 2011, she passed the orbit of Uranus. She was so far from the Sun that it was very dark and cold, and it always felt cozy returning to her slumbers.

Pluto is one of the coldest worlds in the solar system. Its average temperature is a frigid –380°F. That's 380° colder than the inside of your freezer!

New Horizons knew so much about her journey that she was almost her own astronaut! This was essential, because she was so far from Earth that getting help from home took a very long time.

Radio signals travel at 186,000 miles per second, the speed of light. This *sounds* fast. But once *New Horizons* passed the orbit of Uranus, her messages took about two hours to reach Earth. Then, of course, she waited two *more* hours for Earth's reply.

The mission to Pluto was powered partly by plutonium! *Plutonium* is an element that can be used to create electricity—and this is what ran *New Horizons'* computers and instruments.

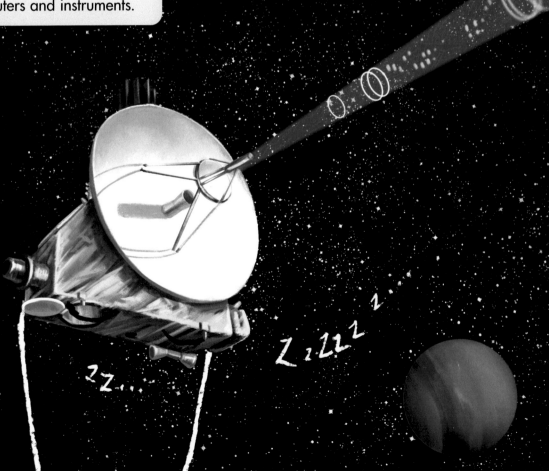

Zz...

Z z Z z z z

Three-and-a-half years after passing Uranus, *New Horizons* crossed the orbit of Neptune. Passing the last planet before Pluto was a huge milestone for the flight and science teams, but the little spacecraft herself snoozed right through it.

A planet's orbit can be either round or *elliptical* (oval). Earth's orbit is fairly round. But Pluto's orbit is so elliptical that its distance from the Sun ranges from 2.7 billion miles to 4.6 billion miles. This means that Pluto is sometimes closer to the Sun than Neptune!*

*Neptune's average distance from the Sun is about 2.8 billion miles.

Six dark and silent months later, *New Horizons* was at Pluto's doorstep—though only in the endless depths of space would millions of miles away be considered "at the doorstep." From this distance, the Sun looked like a very bright star. From here, round-trip contact with Earth took nine hours.

It was December 6, 2014—time for *New Horizons* to wake up and *stay* up.

Alice Bowman, Mission Operations Manager (nicknamed "MOM!")

Dr. Alan Stern, Principal Investigator of the *New Horizons* mission

The flight team began sending detailed instructions for her flyby. Because *New Horizons* was traveling so fast, passing *too* close to Pluto would make her photos blurry. So her team set a "target" distance of 7,800 miles. This was also a good distance for her other instruments to explore Pluto and its moons.

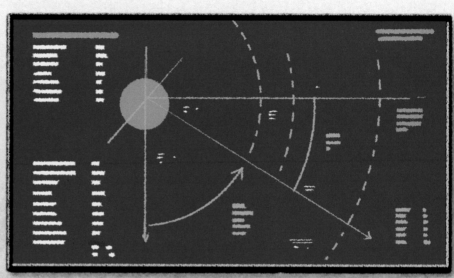

Mission Operations

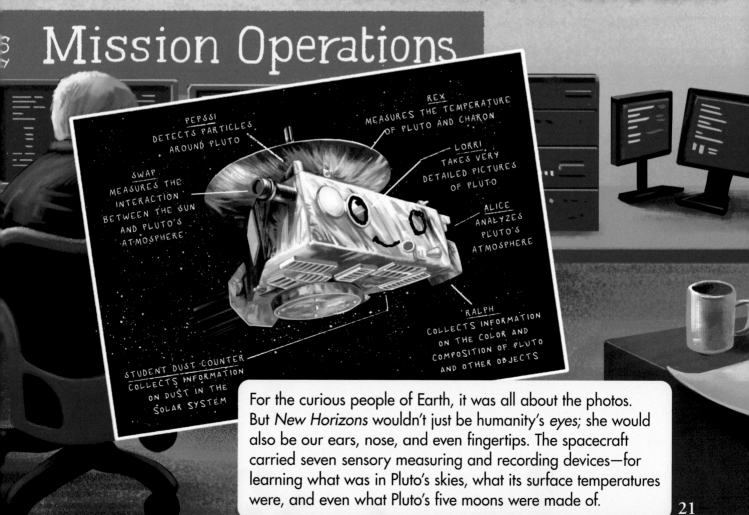

PEPSSI
DETECTS PARTICLES
AROUND PLUTO

REX
MEASURES THE TEMPERATURE
OF PLUTO AND CHARON

SWAP
MEASURES THE
INTERACTION
BETWEEN THE SUN
AND PLUTO'S
ATMOSPHERE

LORRI
TAKES VERY
DETAILED PICTURES
OF PLUTO

ALICE
ANALYZES
PLUTO'S
ATMOSPHERE

RALPH
COLLECTS INFORMATION
ON THE COLOR AND
COMPOSITION OF PLUTO
AND OTHER OBJECTS

STUDENT DUST COUNTER
COLLECTS INFORMATION
ON DUST IN THE
SOLAR SYSTEM

For the curious people of Earth, it was all about the photos. But *New Horizons* wouldn't just be humanity's *eyes*; she would also be our ears, nose, and even fingertips. The spacecraft carried seven sensory measuring and recording devices—for learning what was in Pluto's skies, what its surface temperatures were, and even what Pluto's five moons were made of.

New Horizons started snapping pictures way before her close flyby. And from half a million miles out, she captured a special greeting from Pluto: an enormous, brilliant white "heart," more than 1,000 miles wide!

New Horizons had come three billion miles to see Pluto, and Pluto seemed to be feeling the love.

New Horizons couldn't wait to send Pluto's valentine to Earth! The image took 4½ hours to arrive—but once it did, it set the internet on fire. Everybody loved the dwarf planet with a heart!

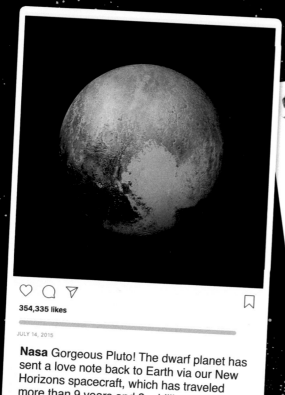

♡ ◯ ◁

354,335 likes

JULY 14, 2015

Nasa Gorgeous Pluto! The dwarf planet has sent a love note back to Earth via our New Horizons spacecraft, which has traveled more than 9 years and 3 + billion miles. This

Eyesonspace @eyesonspace · 7h
Romantic #Pluto ♡ !
Even from 3 billion miles away Pluto knows how to be romantic. The #NewHorizons spacecraft sends #love!

◯ 442   ⇄ 1200   ♡ 120'042   ↥

...izons #nasa

👍❤️😮 124'567

👍 Like   999 Comments

💬 Comment

WE ♥ PLUTO

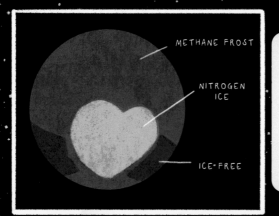

METHANE FROST

NITROGEN ICE

ICE-FREE

Pluto's giant white heart is actually a glacier—but it's made of nitrogen ice, not water ice.

On Earth, nitrogen is a *gas*—an air-like substance. But Pluto is so cold that *its* nitrogen exists mainly as ice. And Pluto's icy heart is the biggest known glacier in the solar system.

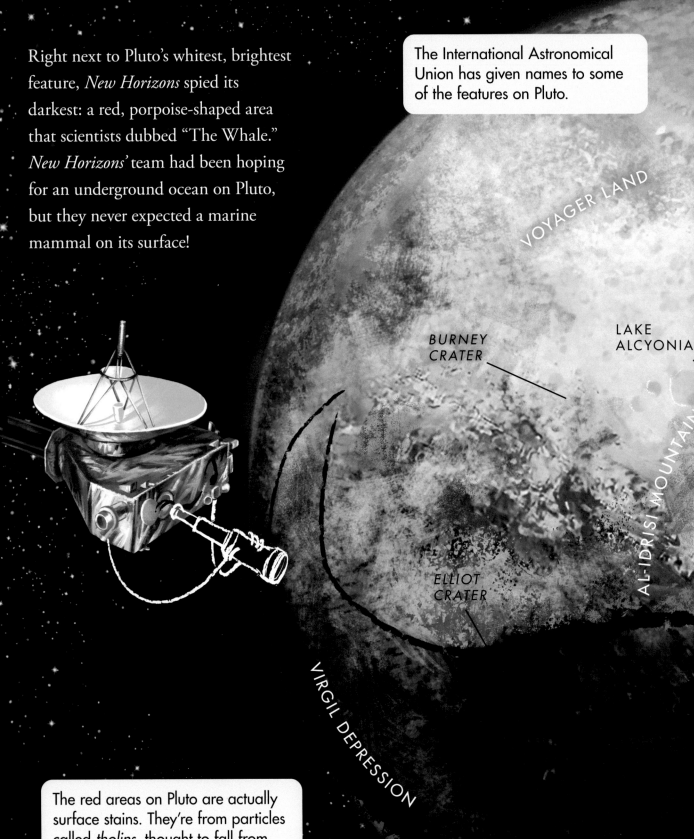

Right next to Pluto's whitest, brightest feature, *New Horizons* spied its darkest: a red, porpoise-shaped area that scientists dubbed "The Whale." *New Horizons'* team had been hoping for an underground ocean on Pluto, but they never expected a marine mammal on its surface!

The International Astronomical Union has given names to some of the features on Pluto.

VOYAGER LAND

BURNEY CRATER

LAKE ALCYONIA

AL-IDRISI MOUNTAIN

ELLIOT CRATER

VIRGIL DEPRESSION

The red areas on Pluto are actually surface stains. They're from particles called *tholins,* thought to fall from Pluto's sky as pink snow.

that a saltwater ocean is hidden deep inside Pluto. This ocean could hold more water than *all* of Earth's seas—certainly enough for Pluto's Whale to take a dive!

HAYABUSA LAND

TARTARUS RIDGES

SPUTNIK PLAIN

TOMBAUGH REGION

HILLARY MOUNTAINS

Finding liquid water on Pluto, even underground, is compelling—because wherever there's water, there's the possibility of life. Pluto probably doesn't have large fish-like creatures, but it might have itty-bitty life forms swimming about.

For a long time, Pluto had been a nearly featureless blob in telescopes. But on July 14, 2015, Pluto suddenly became a *place*. And *New Horizons* couldn't take her cameras off it.

There were towering mountain ranges made entirely of ice. Valleys plunging deeper than the Grand Canyon on Earth. And four neatly spaced dark regions that were nicknamed the "brass knuckles."

6 miles

Pluto is about 70 percent rock and 30 percent ice. Almost all of the rock is massed in Pluto's center, and the ice forms a very thick "shell" around the core.

26

6 miles

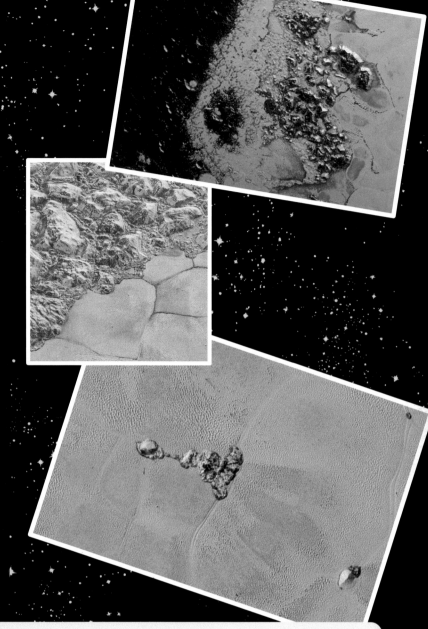

There were "ice blades" the height of New York City skyscrapers, glaciers, craters, and a polar ice cap. There were dunes made not of sand, but of tiny grains of ice. There were ice sheets patterned like tree bark and others that were squeegee-smooth.

Below the equator, *New Horizons* spotted what looked like "ice volcanoes"—volcanoes that spew out icy slush instead of lava. Watching these erupt could be like watching gigantic slushies overflow.

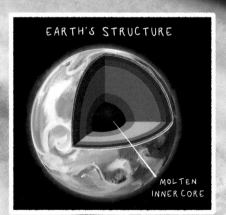

EARTH'S STRUCTURE

MOLTEN INNER CORE

One of *New Horizons'* greatest discoveries is that Pluto is *geologically active,* meaning its landscape is still changing. And scientists can't figure out how this is possible!

For a world to be able to push up mountains or carve canyons, it needs an internal heat source, like a battery inside a toy. Earth's battery is its 10,000°F molten core—but a world as small as Pluto should've lost its heat long ago.

Baffled scientists know *one* thing about Pluto's mystery heat: it's probably related to what's keeping Pluto's underground water ocean from freezing!

New Horizons saw everything clearly, because Pluto's sky was nearly cloudless. And another delight: this alien sky was *blue*!

On Earth, the sky is blue because of our atmosphere. Gases in the sky split sunlight into different colors, and blue light scatters the most, making our daytime sky look blue.

Something like this also happens on Pluto—but Pluto's atmosphere is thinner, with a different mix of gases. So while Pluto's sky is quite dark overhead, around the horizon it's a faint, dreamy blue.

And for *New Horizons,* the sky was *not* the limit.

New Horizons found that Pluto is bigger than previously thought. The extra 50 miles bumped Pluto up from second-largest dwarf planet to the largest.

When *New Horizons* left Earth, her destination was a planet with three moons; but six years later, it was a *dwarf* planet with *five* moons!

That's because, during *New Horizons'* journey, her science team discovered two more moons orbiting Pluto. Tiny *Kerberos* and *Styx* joined mini-moons *Nix* and *Hydra*, and all four orbited Pluto beyond the 800-mile-wide moon, *Charon*.

As *New Horizons* photographed Charon, she discovered something else: the big moon's north pole was the exact same red color as Pluto's Whale!

Scientists suspect that a gas called *methane* escapes from Pluto's atmosphere and flows to nearby Charon. This methane freezes to Charon's icy pole, and sunlight transforms it into the same reddish particles found on Pluto. No other worlds are known to share an atmosphere this way—and it probably happens because Pluto and Charon are just 12,000 miles apart.

But *New Horizons'* most stunning photo
came as she was taking her leave: Pluto,
lit from behind by the Sun, was
"crowned" with the hazy blue glow
of its atmosphere. This was one
of the last pictures of Pluto
New Horizons took during
her flyby, and it was a
glorious farewell.

New Horizons—
with help from her
Earth team—had
done it! She'd
voyaged an
incredible three
billion miles and
hit her small target
area precisely. As
Alan Stern, leader
of the *New Horizons*
mission, said, it was
"the equivalent of
hitting a golf ball in
New York and landing
it in a soup can in
California!"*

*Alan Stern and David Ginspoon,
*Chasing New Horizons: Inside the Epic
First Mission to Pluto* (New York: Picador,
2018), p. 187.

The spacecraft had also gathered so much data on Pluto that it would take her 16 months to send it all home.

But *New Horizons'* story wasn't over.

Even as she was sending Pluto data back to Earth, she was headed for another, even *more* distant world. It was Kuiper Belt object *Arrokoth*, which hadn't even been discovered when *New Horizons* was launched!

New Horizons would reach Arrokoth on New Year's Day, 2019.

She had another billion miles to go.

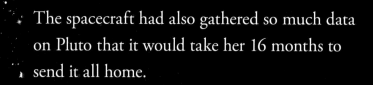

New Year's Day, 2019:

Arrokoth!

In the earliest minutes of 2019, *New Horizons* reached Arrokoth. This faraway world was like nothing ever seen!

In its first photos, Arrokoth resembled a reddish snowman. But seen from the side, it was "flattened," like lumpy pancakes.

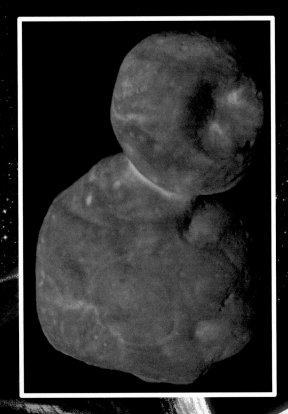

Scientists think that Arrokoth formed from two snowball-soft worldlets that collided, then hardened together.

Arrokoth is only about 22 miles long. But because it hasn't changed since its "birth," it's teaching us a lot about the solar system's early years. Information continues to flow in. In fact, *New Horizons* remains so robust that her team wants to visit an even *more* distant Kuiper Belt world in the 2020s!

And nobody doubts that the little spacecraft could.

Journey Timeline

January 19, 2006

New Horizons blasts off from Cape Canaveral, Florida, and, nine hours later, passes the Moon

April 7, 2006

New Horizons passes the orbit of Mars, fourth planet from the Sun

August 24, 2006

Astronomers suggest that Pluto should be called a "dwarf planet," though planetary scientists strongly disagree

February 28, 2007

New Horizons makes its closest approach to Jupiter—1.4 million miles—and receives a "speed boost" from the planet's enormous gravity

June 8, 2008

New Horizons passes the orbit of Saturn, sixth planet from the Sun

March 18, 2011

New Horizons passes the orbit of Uranus, seventh planet from the Sun

July 20, 2011

New Horizons' team announces the discovery of a fourth moon (*Kerberos*) orbiting Pluto

July 11, 2012

New Horizons' team announces the discovery of a fifth moon (*Styx*) orbiting Pluto

August 25, 2014

New Horizons passes the orbit of Neptune, eighth planet from the Sun and the last planet before Pluto

July 14, 2015

Plutopalooza! *New Horizons* makes its historic flyby of Pluto and sends Earth the first-ever close-up pictures of this distant world!

September, 2015

New Horizons sets out for Arrokoth, a small rocky world a billion miles past Pluto in the Kuiper Belt

January 1, 2019

New Horizons flies past Arrokoth, which becomes the most distant world ever explored by humans!

Glossary

AIR RESISTANCE The *slowing* effect that's created when a flying object rubs against air

ARROKOTH A tiny, oddly shaped worldlet about a billion miles past Pluto. This object's official name is *2014 MU69*; its nickname, Arrokoth, means "sky" in the Native American Powhatan language. (Upon its discovery, Arrokoth was temporarily nicknamed *Ultima Thule*, but it was officially nicknamed *Arrokoth* in November 2019.)

ASTEROID A space rock that orbits the Sun but isn't big enough to be a planet or dwarf planet

(THE) ASTEROID BELT A ring of asteroids that circles the Sun between the orbits of Mars and Jupiter. The asteroid belt also includes one dwarf planet, *Ceres.*

ATMOSPHERE The layer of gases surrounding a world. Earth's atmosphere is *air*, a mixture of nitrogen and oxygen. Pluto's atmosphere consists of nitrogen, methane, and carbon monoxide.

BINARY PLANET (or *"double planet"*) A planet-moon pair, where both bodies are of roughly similar size

CANYON A deep cut in the surface of a moon or planet

CERES (pronounced *"series"*) The only dwarf planet in the asteroid belt

CHARON (pronounced *"Sharon"*) The largest of Pluto's five moons. At 751 miles wide, Charon is half as wide as Pluto.

COMET A chunk of ice and dust that orbits the Sun, usually very far from Earth

CRATER A bowl-shaped "scar" that marks the spot where an asteroid or comet crashed onto a world

DWARF PLANET A rounded object in outer space

EARTH The only planet in the solar system known to have life

GAS An invisible, air-like substance that can expand to fill any volume or shape

GLACIER A large mass of slowly moving ice

GRAVITY A force that "pulls" objects toward the center of a planet or another massive object

GRAVITY ASSIST The use of a planet's (or another object's) gravitational "pull" to change a spacecraft's speed or direction during a flyby

HIBERNATION (as used in space exploration) When all non-essential systems in a spacecraft are switched off temporarily, to save wear and tear on the spacecraft's instruments and components

HYDRA A small, irregularly shaped moon orbiting Pluto. Hydra was discovered in 2005.

ICE VOLCANO A volcano that erupts icy water slush instead of lava

JUPITER The fifth planet from the Sun and the largest planet in the solar system

KERBEROS A tiny, irregularly shaped moon orbiting Pluto. Kerberos was discovered in 2012 (with the Hubble Space Telescope), after *New Horizons* had left Earth.

KUIPER BELT (pronounced *"KY-per Belt"*) A ring of comets, asteroids, and at least ten dwarf planets that orbits the solar system beyond Neptune. The Kuiper Belt is similar to the asteroid belt, but much larger and farther from the Sun. It's named for renowned astronomer Gerard Kuiper.

LAVA Hot, molten rock that can flow like a river

MARS The fourth planet from the Sun, and the planet whose surface is most like Earth's

METHANE A colorless, odorless gas found on many planets and moons

MOON An object that orbits another, larger object in space. (Whenever "moon" is spelled with a capital "M," it refers to *Earth's* Moon, which is 2,159 miles wide and about 239,000 miles away from Earth.)

MOONLET A very small moon orbiting a planet or dwarf planet

NEPTUNE The eighth planet from the Sun and the fourth-largest planet in the solar system

NEW HORIZONS The first spacecraft ever to travel to Pluto and to a Kuiper Belt object. *New Horizons* left Earth on January 19, 2006, and arrived at Pluto on July 14, 2015—a journey of 9½ years.

NIX A small, irregularly shaped moon orbiting Pluto. Nix was discovered in 2005.

ORBIT To move in a path around another object. An orbit can be either circular, oval-shaped ("elliptical"), or U-shaped (called a "hyperbolic" orbit). Earth's orbit is nearly circular; Pluto's orbit is very elliptical.

PLANET A large, round object that orbits a star; its roundness is due to its mass.

PLANETARY SCIENTIST A scientist who deals with the planets, asteroids, comets, and Kuiper Belt objects of the solar system, particularly planets and moons

PLUTO The solar system's ninth planet, and the first dwarf planet discovered in the Kuiper Belt

PLUTONIUM An element that can be used to create electricity. Plutonium was actually named after Pluto!

POLAR ICE CAP A dome-shaped area of ice at a planet's north or south pole

ROBOTIC Being able to replicate certain human functions automatically

SATURN The sixth planet from the Sun, and the second-largest planet in the solar system

SOLAR SYSTEM A star (such as our Sun) plus all the planets and objects that orbit it

SPACECRAFT A machine that travels in space

STAR A huge ball of extremely hot gas in space, powered by nuclear fusion. The star that's closest to Earth is the Sun. All other stars are so far away that they look like tiny points of light.

STYX A tiny, irregularly shaped moon orbiting Pluto. Styx was discovered in 2012 (with the Hubble Space Telescope), after *New Horizons* had left Earth.

(THE) SUN The star at the center of our solar system

TELESCOPE A tool that makes faraway objects look larger and clearer

THOLINS Reddish organic particles that exist on icy worlds in the outer solar system

URANUS The seventh planet from the Sun, and the third-largest planet in the solar system

VOLCANO A landform (usually a mountain) where hot, melted rock erupts through the surface of a planet

(THE) WHALE An enormous, red, whale-shaped feature on Pluto's surface

Suggestions for Further Reading

Buckley, James Jr. *Curious About Pluto*. New York: Grosset & Dunlap, 2016.

Glaser, Chayer. *Pluto: The Icy Dwarf Planet (Out of This World)*. New York: Bearport, 2015.

Kahn, Katie. *A Space Explorer's Guide to Pluto (Volume 9)*. Seattle: CreateSpace, 2015.

Kortenkamp, Steve. *Demoting Pluto: The Discovery of the Dwarf Planets*. North Mankato, MN: Capstone, 2015.

Stern, Alan, and David Grinspoon. *Chasing New Horizons: Inside the Epic First Mission to Pluto*. New York: Picador, 2018.

Taylor-Butler, Christine. *Pluto: Dwarf Planet* (Updated). New York: Scholastic Press, 2005 & 2008.

Wade, Stef. *A Place for Pluto*. North Mankato, MN: Capstone, 2018.

Weitekamp, Margaret A. *Pluto's Secret*. New York: Abrams Books for Young Readers, 2013.

Selected Bibliography

Bow, James. *New Horizons: A Robot Explores Pluto and the Kuiper Belt*. New York: PowerKids Press, 2017.

Carson, Mary Kay. *Mission to Pluto: The First Visit to an Ice Dwarf and the Kuiper Belt*. Boston/New York: Houghton Mifflin Harcourt, 2016.

Keeter, Bill. "One Year Later: New Horizons' Top 10 Discoveries at Pluto." *NASA TV*, July 14, 2016. https://www.nasa.gov/feature/one-year-later-new-horizons-top-10-discoveries-at-pluto.

Scott, Elaine. *To Pluto & Beyond: The Amazing Voyage of New Horizons*. New York: Viking, 2018.